29 Days to L.O.V.E. Literacy

Dr. K. Childs

29 Days to L.O.V.E. Literacy

Copyright © 2016 by Dr. K. Childs and Ed|Whys

All rights reserved. No part of this book may be reproduced or transmitted in any form or by any means whatsoever, including photocopying, recording or by any information storage and retrieval system, without written permission from the publisher and/or author. Contact: Ed|Whys PO Box 751631, Houston, TX 77275-1631.

Cover Art: Heart logo is a Trademark of Dr. K. Childs, Ed|Whys, and DESIGN:WHYS.

All other images, illustrations, and trademarks are property of the respective copyright holders. Royalty Free Images and Illustrations from Pixabay. www.pixabay.com

29 Days to L.O.V.E. Literacy

Table of Contents

1
INTRODUCTION

6
LEARNING
Day 1 - Day 5

11
OPPORTUNITY
Day 6 - Day 12

18
VALUED
Day 13 - Day 18

24
ENHANCED
Day 19 - Day 29

35
L.O.V.E
Conclusion

36
ABOUT THE AUTHOR

38
APPENDIX
Appendix A: Letter From Oprah

Dr. K. Childs

29 Days to L.O.V.E. Literacy

Dedication

Dedicated to my parents for inspiring me to read without knowing it—from them bringing in the Sunday newspaper every week into the home, and me watching them read it...to my dad asking me as a young girl to read various signs and sayings inside and outside the house... and for briefly subscribing to a book and magazine club for kids for me. Thank you for fostering a love of reading- as it fueled me to want to write, and ALWAYS read anything that I can get my hands on—even reading the fine print.

Dr. K. Childs

29 Days to L.O.V.E. Literacy

Preface

Learning, Opportunity, Valued, and Enhanced (L.O.V.E) was created initially as a way to celebrate literacy during the month of February (which happened to fall during a leap year on this occasion). However, it can be implemented any time of the year.

On each day listed, there is literacy learning advice or teaching tips, as well as an accompanying resource to help students foster a love for literacy in the areas of reading, writing, listening, and speaking. The content shared, will be applicable to varying ages of students, and will use an array of materials to hone in on skills that students will need to grow their vocabularies, increase their comprehension and critical thinking, and many other necessary learning tasks.

Dr. K. Childs

29 Days to L.O.V.E. Literacy

INTRODUCTION

Literacy skills (reading, writing, speaking, and listening) are such a crucial part of any students' education. As educators (and parents) we want our students to be fully literate, and learn concepts in general core subjects such as math, science, history, etc. In order to do this, they must have the ability to communicate and take in new knowledge using their literacy skills. We have heard popular statements such as "reading is fundamental", but to what extent are we teaching our students this? Do we only want them to know "how" to read? Or should we be striving towards showing them the necessity of the skill beyond basic comprehension?

As a former 5th and 6th grade teacher for many years, I often received students at the start of a new school year who were fed up with reading and writing, or perhaps they never liked it in the first place. That's right. Fifth graders who thought they had reading and writing all figured out—because the "test" (state assessment) said they were "Commended". They had no desire to learn more English and Language Arts curriculum because they "know how to read". I

INTRODUCTION

also had others who had simply lost interest. Students in primary grades are provided with interactive games, plays, read-alouds, songs, thematic units, and integrated activities, and then once they reach their middle years, the challenge of learning new literacy skills is no longer "fun". The curriculum often changes, and students have no desire to keep building their learning. That loss of interest or lack of motivation to read has been studied, and is commonly known as a "slump" (Chall, 1983, 1996) that happens as early as third grade in many students. No one quite knows when it happens (as each student is different), nor does this happen with all students. But one thing is for sure, we must address this issue, and get our students to know the importance of their literacy foundation and CONTINUED development.

L.O.V.E.

INTRODUCTION

This short instructional manual, will provide activities that are categorized with the titles of Learning, Opportunity, Valued, and Enhanced. Although many of the activities provided overlap into more than one category, they are all equally important in getting students engaged in literary concepts.

Learning

Literacy learning must include a combination of motivation and innovative repetition of skills. Learning should always be a chance to fine-tune knowledge. Lastly, learning should contain opportunities to explore concepts- new and old.

Opportunity

Building a strong literacy foundation promotes exposure to additional education opportunities. A child/student that is literate has the opportunity to produce and be exposed to creative works. It allows a student the opportunity to transcend and explore the world and their surroundings. The improvement of literacy skills is always a learning opportunity.

INTRODUCTION

When building a literacy foundation, we should be in search of learning opportunities and resources that are simple to implement and put into practice.

Valued

Learning new literary skills must be an experience that students can have some ownership in. Students can be entertained (at times fairly easily), but they must also see the value of the skills that we teach them. They must see the value of learning grammar rules, creating and formulating opinions, comprehending text (for fiction and non-fiction purposes), inferring texts, drawing conclusions and many other skills that we work on over the course of their academic years. Making connections to their experiences and the importance of the skills they are learning is essential.

Enhanced

Literacy learning should be an experience that builds and enhances a student's natural abilities, and always provide room for improvement.

INTRODUCTION

Writing, reading, speaking and listening are skills that can forever be sharpened. Incorporating technology, modifying language/key terms, building an extensive vocabulary, and personalization of instruction are just small pieces of how skills can be enhanced. Lessons and skills related to reading and writing should always offer room to explore, and leave room to extend steps higher in order for students to grow, reach, and explore at another time. Skills should never be introduced in isolation without a clear path of guiding students to a place where they are motivated to improve.

References

Chall, J.S. (1983). Stages of reading development, New York: McGraw-Hill.

Chall, J. S. (1996). Stages of reading development (2nd ed.). Fort Worth, Tex.: Harcourt Brace.

LEARNING

 **DAY 1**

Close Reading
Teach students to L.O.V.E. Literacy, by sharing the importance of re-reading information, and how to "close" read. Close (Pronounced cloze) reading is simply the ability to re-read carefully, and in a purposeful manner.

Activity
Use Oreo cookies to teach these skills. More information on this mini lesson can be found on Who's Who and New blog. (This is not my own activity, but it's a great idea! Besides, how can you go wrong with Oreos?)

DAY 2

Vocabulary

Who doesn't like to learn new, questionable, "is that an actual word" vocabulary words? Building a strong and diverse vocabulary not only gives students confidence in reading and writing, but also helps with their verbal communication.

Activity

Add a spark to literacy skills by building up vocabulary one day at a time! Using a calendar (print or digital), at the beginning of the month, designate a day to learn one new word. Write or type them on the calendar. The words do not necessarily need to be English and Language Arts based - expand your child's/students' vocabulary with words from various fields and subject areas (Math, Science, History, Music and the Arts). Check out Vocabulary.com Top 1,000 Words. There are 1,000 words to keep almost anyone, of any age busy.

LEARNING

DAY 3

What's Your Opinion?
Promote the L.O.V.E. of literacy by having your child/student begin to work on formulating opinions, and the ability to think critically.

Activity
Have your child/student write a review on something that they have experienced (This experience could be a review of a video game, toy, shoes, or clothing items). They could also review places they have visited, such as a museum, a restaurant, or a vacation destination. For a bit of inspiration, view this article: "Twelve Year-Old Entrepreneur Launches Travel Review Website for Kids"

LEARNING

DAY 4 ♥

Let's go to the Movies
Get your child/student to L.O.V.E. Literacy by using movies to explain the important elements of plot, and parts of a traditional essay. Students should understand the importance of introductions and conclusions, and visualization in reading and writing.

Activity
For practice with understanding introductions, choose a well known movie that most students have seen (or have the student select their own), and have them write an introduction as if they are creating a movie trailer. Have them write the "preview", and then draw or explain the visuals which they would use. This could be done with conclusions, and it would be treated as a "review" of the movie.

LEARNING

 **DAY 5**

Using Cartoons to Infer
L.O.V.E literacy by teaching students the concept of inference. This is a skill that builds as a child develops more background knowledge.

Activity
Have your child/student watch a few scenes from old "Roadrunner" cartoons. Once they have a grasp of the characters and their roles, have them watch clips. Then cut the clip off at a point of "rising action." Have them infer the next actions of the coyote and the roadrunner on paper or verbally.

OPPORTUNITY

DAY 6

Get inspired by boredom

A common problem that causes students to not L.O.V.E. literacy–BOREDOM. If you have a child/student who gets "bored" while reading, they might not be able to make a connection to what they are reading.

Activities

1. Have them compare and contrast settings by inviting them to compare their own environment with those in the story.

2. Have the child/student "doodle" or make illustrations while reading (either on the text, or a separate sheet of paper). With older students, this option can later be modified and used as a "note-taking skills" lesson.

3. If reading non-fiction or expository text, pick a small element to research (even if simply giving the students a short 3-5 minute break from the text to look up information).

OPPORTUNITY

 DAY 7

Hearing It

Close reading has been a very "hot" topic in recent years. Have your child/student put a spin on close reading with digital tools.

Activity

Instead of simply re-reading for understanding, have students use a tool such the Adobe Spark app (available on iOS only) to record and work through the purpose of the reading, the arrangement of the text, and specific vocabulary words. Using the app, they can record their voice, and provide text and pictures or illustrations.

DAY 8

Library and Bookstore Tours

Help your child/student fall in L.O.V.E with literacy by encouraging them to read and write, by being open and willing to broaden their print environment at home and wherever resources are available. Show your child/student the wide range of learning opportunities that reading and writing can present to them.

Activity

Library and Bookstore Tours: Routine and consistency are important. However, to keep students engaged and presented with a variety of materials, take your child/student to different libraries or bookstores. Don't always go to the same places to find materials to buy or checkout. Make a schedule, and build anticipation. If transportation is an issue, encourage your child/student to move to a different section of the library while at school. Even try venturing into resources such as e-books or audio books for a different approach. Bottom line, have a plan when looking for reading materials, but don't be afraid to make simple changes that could make a HUGE impact.

 **DAY 9**

Lyrics
Move beyond using music to solely memorize facts or concepts. A favorite song, might not only be therapeutic, but it can also be used to develop literacy skills. From modern day pop, to classic rock, to "doo wop", the lyrics of a song can be used to learn concepts such as tone, vocabulary, theme, and comprehension.

Activity
Have your child/student write a critical analysis of a song's lyrics. Have them share and compare their perspective with another student or even an audience. For younger students, use lyrics or specific songs to teach emotions or adjectives.

DAY 10

Letter Writing

Send it in a letter! With letter writing, not only will your child/student work on their handwriting skills, but they will be able to think critically (by formulating questions), and give their ideas and thoughts a sense of purpose. You will be teaching them that literacy is not only a form of gaining and learning information, but it is also a process of communication.

Activity

Have your child/student write letters to someone whom they admire. It could be a well known author, celebrity figure, or someone in their community, family or home environment. Don't stop with one letter, send several- make a habit out of it. The treat in doing this activity is the possibility of a response being received–as was the case my sophomore year in high school. In 1995, after writing a high school assignment to someone I felt was influential, I shockingly received a letter back from Oprah that I still have to this day. See also: An Introduction to Letter Writing via Reading Rockets.

OPPORTUNITY

 DAY 11

News

Challenge young and old writers in your family to write for news or informational purposes. Summarization and research are key skills that are necessary for a solid literacy foundation.

Activity

If writing in a classroom setting, challenge your students to create a classroom newsletter. For an even better twist, have students (or your child if you are a parent) create a weekly or monthly "family newsletter". Newsletters are good informational sources, and it would be a great document to look back on in the future.

DAY 12

Dramas & Plays
L.O.V.E Literacy by giving your child/student the opportunity to read plays and dramas. Students of all ages love the excitement of hearing their peers read and portray a new character. Plays and dramas work on elements of literature such as plot, setting, tone, climax, captions, stage directions, and even speech/speaking.

Activity
Try to find plays that represent historical events and historical figures. My students particularly loved learning the story of Fannie Lou Hamer, in the play "A Long Road to Freedom" (Scholastic). You can also find an abundance of great reads at "50 Classic Plays that Every Student Should Read" (OnlineCollegeCourses.com)

VALUED

♥ DAY 13

Career

Help your child/student gain an understanding that literacy not only effects them in the classroom, but in career and employment settings as well. Even entry level positions require certain skills that are developed with a strong sense of literacy.

Activity

Have your child/student brainstorm a list of jobs and career settings on a piece of paper. On the opposite side, have them write down specific literacy skills needed for each job. This could be done with younger children, or second language learners by illustrating a predetermined list of literacy tasks that are used in specific jobs. If done in a classroom, this could be charted and used as a comparison between different careers. A great website for kids (grades K-8) to search career related information is Kids.gov

Fight Boredom

Do you have readers who are bored or lose focus when reading? L.O.V.E literacy by making reading a bit more interesting and realistic. Teach children/students to put themselves and their experiences in a story which they are currently reading. They can even go as far as changing the names of characters to names of people whom they know.

Activity

Have students rewrite or retell a story that has already been written, and change the story so that it contains the settings and people who impact the students in their environment. Need super creative topics? Try using Scholastic's Story Starters for a fun twist for students in grades K-6.

♥ DAY 15

Will I use this?
Students building their literacy skills might not L.O.V.E. literacy, due to the content or subject matter not being relevant to them or their future. Students need to know that they are learning literacy skills that will be with them for their entire academic careers, and in whatever field they choose to make a career of.

Activity
Students often learn vocabulary in school, but we do not understand how the terms/vocabulary apply to our daily lives and careers. Have your child/student select a career and list five vocabulary terms that relate to that career (ex. Patient, Prescription, Chart, Cardiovascular, and Digestive). Have the student use the five terms to create a paragraph introducing themselves, as a member of that profession.

VALUED

DAY 16 ♥

Favorite Things
L.O.V.E. literacy by showing your child/student how writing and reading relates to their favorite things- whether it be movies, music, or games— someone had to construct some type of writing in order to produce their favorite products or pastimes.

Activity
If your child/student loves to watch movies or television, encourage them to write a play, mini-sitcom, or cartoon script. If their interest is music, encourage them to write lyrics. Hip hop is a widely popular genre among younger and older students. Hip hop (clean lyrics) can be used to teach elements of writing poetry. It also can be used to express thoughts, and memorize key concepts. If your child/student is into gaming (online or board games), encourage them to write game reviews, summaries of the main point (theme), or directions to playing the game for a player who is new to the game (descriptive writing and process).

VALUED

 **DAY 17**

Reverse Psychology
You often hear of children/students who do not like to write. Most only prefer to write about what they like. Use a bit of reverse psychology with them, in order to get them to see the ease of the writing process.

Activity
Discuss with the students what they find difficult with the writing process. Take down the information they communicate with you as pre-writing. Put the information that they share with you in a web, or some sort of graphic organizer. Use this as an opportunity to show the process of organization in writing. Do this by putting their reasons for disliking writing in story or essay format. Show them that although writing usually has a set process, they have the freedom to express their own (often creative) thoughts.

DAY 18

Meeting of the Minds
Students need to be able to express their opinions and thoughts in multiple manners, such as speaking (not just in writing).

Activity
Get your children/students to L.O.V.E. reading by coming together (or with you as a parent) at a set time every week (or two weeks, etc), and share books, magazines, or online/electronic books that they have read. Create a certain amount of resources the students must bring to the table, and set criteria of what information they will share during the "round-table". They can then either swap resources, or create a reading "Wish List" based off of what was shared.

ENHANCED

 **DAY 19**

Poetry
L.O.V.E Literacy by having your children/students write a poem or song lyric. Music is a great way to get a child/student to make a connection with poetry.

Activity
Have your child/student write a poem about love. It does not have to be about "romantic" love, but love in a caring and endearing manner. Poems could be as simple as writing an acrostic or a haiku, or a couplet. If you choose to use lyrics instead of poetry, use lyrics that have already been written— use that as an opportunity to teach elements such as mood, word choice, adjectives, patterns, and sentence structure.

ENHANCED

DAY 20

Literacy Jar
Many children/students often only read what they "like". Their minds and opinions are often shaped based off of what is presented to them in the classroom, and at home (if reading and literacy is even a focus at home).

Activity
Create a jar or box in which you put the names of various literary genres (ex. Fiction, Non-Fiction, Narrative, Biography, Poetry, etc.). Draw out a name of a genre each week, and focus on reading a different genre each week. Depending on their age, set a goal for how many books, articles, or pages to read each week.

ENHANCED

 DAY 21

Journals and Blogs, oh my!
Familiarity Rules! Students like writing about what is familiar. Family and friends and their environment are what they know the MOST about.

Activity
Invite your child/student to write at least once per week about topics related to their experience in their family, and friendships. This could be placed into a journal, or you could even turn this process into a personal blog of some sort (check privacy settings). If in a classroom setting (with parent permission), feature the stories of students in an area where others can view them (only if the stories don't contain confidential information, and aren't too personal). For teachers, try using sites such as Edmodo.

DAY 22

Variety of materials
L.O.V.E Literacy by letting your children/students read from sources other than textbooks. Magazines and comics are sources of print that contain information that are creative and full of imagery and visuals. Reading such materials not only sparks interest, but allows students to become comfortable with different types of genres and styles of literacy.

Activity
Challenge the child to read at least 2 different types of print materials per week. Chart the progress, and determine your child's/students' favorite genre.

♥ DAY 23

Voice

Students need to understand the importance of "voice" in writing and reading. They practice this all of the time when watching TV, particularly cartoons– there are often "voice overs" that perfectly demonstrate what characters think or feel.

Activity

For writing, choose a passage from a simple story (ex. a nursery rhyme or fair tale) that has a strong main character. Have them re-write a certain line of that story, using different and opposite tones and emotions.

For reading, have the students listen to a story, and create signs or signals (paper, faces or hand signs) to identify certain tones or emotions.

ENHANCED

DAY 24 ♥

Tech Tools for Learning

L.O.V.E. literacy by using apps! Help your child/student learn to read by not only giving them an electronic device for "fun" or to keep them quiet, but to help them with reading comprehension skills.

Activity

Use the thousands of phone and tablet apps that are available in various formats, to start helping your child/student learn skills at a young age, and continue with more challenging applications. The key to using apps for students to learn, is that you must know the purpose of using the app, and to not just put your child/student on them without expressing the objective or guiding them. Reading Rockets has a good list with some really good suggestions for Reading Comprehension applications.

Dr. K. Childs

DAY 25

Create Your Own Fairy-Tale

Most children/students love fantasy stories and fairy tales. The imagination and imagery in these stories draw children to "believe" in these stories —no matter how ridiculous or far-fetched the stories might be.

Activity

Work with students on voice, character traits, plot, setting, drawing conclusions, and many other skills by having your child/student create their OWN fairy tale– based off of the traditional elements in the fairy tale and fantasy genre. However, to make their stories unique, have them put their own "spin" on a traditional story. Invite the child/student to implement elements of their life, culture, and environment in their writing. For some inspiration, use Fairy Tales Gone Wild: 10 Creative Ways to Teach Fairy Tales by Erin Macpherson via weareteachers.com BONUS Tip: Fairy tales and fantasy genres are not just for young students!

ENHANCED

DAY 26 ♥

Say It Out Loud

Say it loud! Reading aloud doesn't always mean reading in front of a group of students or peers. It is important to read aloud to model pronunciation, and very helpful in working on fluency.

Activity

Have your children/students read together in a small group with peers. Another possibility is to have them read with an elderly or well respected family member that they may not always get to spend "learning time" with. Reading is not always an independent task- it can be a team effort, and children/students should not feel as if they are "own their own" in developing literacy.

ENHANCED

 DAY 27

Daily How To's

Students should learn the importance of reading and following directions. Comprehension of events in a story, and paying attention to sequence are important in learning to be an effective reader.

Activity

Have your child/student write directions for a particular process that they go through every day. For example, how to tie your shoe, how to play a certain game/sport, or how to brush your teeth. For those who are older, they can share processes related to their education, how to drive a car, or how to apply for a job.

ENHANCED

DAY 28 ♥

History Year-Round
Students in school are often encouraged to read about specific racial or ethic groups during the months that are designated as "History" or "Heritage" months (Ex. Black, Hispanic, Asian, Native American History, Women's History, etc.).

Activity
Use the resources that are shared on various websites and media outlets, throughout the year- not just on the chosen month. Extend knowledge beyond celebrations—just because a month ends or a month is over, the learning about marginalized groups should not stop.

Dr. K. Childs

♥ DAY 29

Integration Across Subjects

On the last day in this journey, it is most important, to teach your child/student to L.O.V.E. literacy by showing them the importance of reading and writing in all of the subjects that they learn in school (even Mathematics, History, and Sciences), and throughout their lives. The literacy skills that they learn, are their foundation for everything else they will learn. Reading and writing is used to gain further knowledge, and share knowledge. It is a small set of skills which allows us to explore and engage in a large world.

CONCLUSION

Thank you for "loving" literacy with me!
My philosophy of teaching supports inquiry, and personalization of learning. It will be left up to you to determine and find what works, and what will be successful for your child or student. The hope is that we continue to build a world of readers, writers, and thinkers, that love a good book and literacy in all forms.

ABOUT THE AUTHOR

Dr. K. Childs is a native of Wichita, Kansas. A product of Wichita USD #259 Public Schools (K-12), her college studies took her to Wichita State University (1 year), and to Kansas State University– where in 2002 she earned a Bachelor of Science in Elementary Education (ESL Concentration), and a Master of Science in Curriculum and Instruction (Reading and Language Arts) in 2004. She earned a Doctorate of Education in Curriculum and Instruction from Texas Southern University in Houston, Texas in May 2013.

Dr. K. Childs has taught in public schools in both Kansas and Texas. Her pre-service experience included working in various capacities as a tutor

ABOUT THE AUTHOR

and paraprofessional in the K-6 setting. She was a 5th and 6th grade teacher for eleven years. Dr. K. Childs has taught all subjects, but her specialty area is English Language Arts and Reading.

Working in an ESL setting for her entire career has allowed her to have exposure to a variety of ethnic backgrounds and experience with students that have spoken over twelve different languages. Having such diverse students, she has had to be flexible and accommodating to the various needs of her students. Dr. K. Childs takes pride in making curriculum interesting, relevant, and meaningful.

She was a first generation college student, and would like to give back to other students by sharing knowledge she lacked. Dr. K. Childs was previously an Adjunct Faculty member in Developmental Education at San Jacinto College (South) in Houston, Texas. Dr. K. Childs is currently a faculty member in the College of Education at Texas Southern University in Houston, Texas.

Beyond education, Dr. Childs has always had a love for music, and enjoys singing, traveling, reading, writing, and working on various projects with her husband, with whom she currently resides with in Houston, Texas.

 **APPENDIX A**

October 6, 1995

Wichita, KS

Dear Kamshia,

Thank you for writing and watching The Oprah Winfrey Show.

I appreciate your letter and hope that you will continue working hard in school. Keep up your grades -- education is the key to success!

Wishing you the best,

Oprah Winfrey
OW/sg

P O BOX 909715
CHICAGO ILLINOIS 60690

Dr. K. Childs

Lightning Source UK Ltd.
Milton Keynes UK
UKHW02f0933310718
326552UK00008B/254/P